ACEDIA ALBION
AVATAR FASHION
Vol.VII

Copyright © 2008 Acedia Albion

Produced by Studio SFO 3145 Geary #713 San Francisco CA 94118

All rights reserved under Pan American and International Copyright Conventions. Without limiting the rights under copyright reserved above, no part of this publication may be reproduced, stored in, or introduced into a retrieval system, or transmitted, in any form or by any means (electronic, mechanical, photo copying, recording or otherwise), without prior written permission of both the copyright owner and the above publisher of the book.

The greatest care has been taken in compiling this book. However, no responsibility can be accepted by the publishers or compilers for the accuracy of the information presented.

Manufactured in the United States of America.

Albion, Acedia. 2008

Avatar Fashion Volume VII.

ISBN 978-0-6151-5343-8

AVATAR FASHION VOLUME VII

Welcome to the world of Avatar Fashion. Throughout seven volumes Acedia Albion has documented the emerging age of the avatar.
A world where anything is possible, where we live digitally, where stories are played out, and where styles change in extremely fast cycles.
This volume features Acedia Albion's fashion and photography spanning 2007 and 2008.

Standing on the verge of a new stage in virtual worlds, looking as always into the future and what we can become...this is Avatar Fashion!

AVATAR FASHION 2008

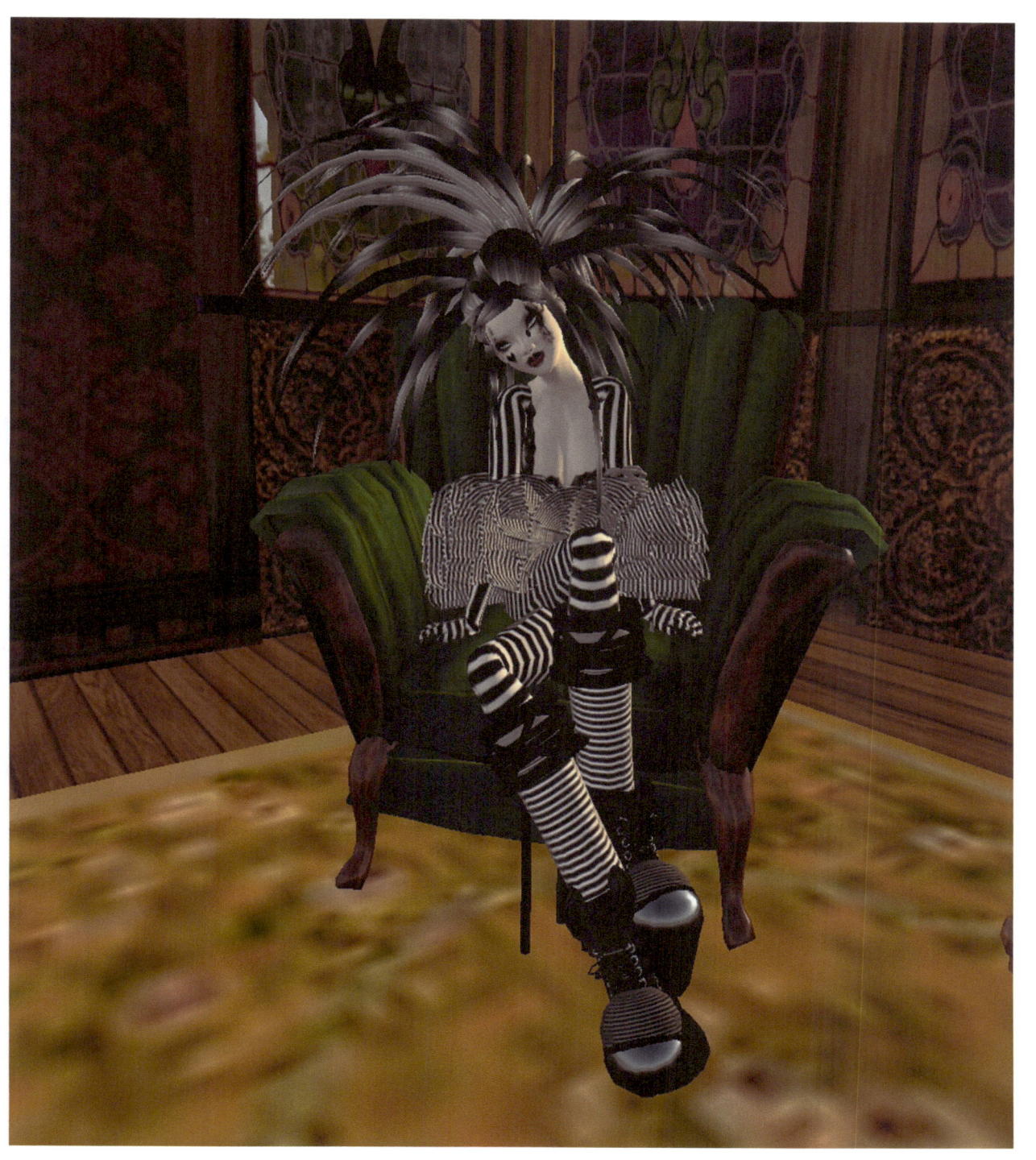

AVATAR FASHION 2008

AVATAR FASHION 2008

AVATAR FASHION 2008

AVATAR FASHION 2008

AVATAR FASHION 2008

AVATAR FASHION 2008

AVATAR FASHION 2008

AVATAR FASHION 2008

AVATAR FASHION 2008

AVATAR FASHION 2008

AVATAR FASHION 2008

AVATAR FASHION 2008

AVATAR FASHION 2008

AVATAR FASHION 2008

AVATAR FASHION 2008

AVATAR FASHION 2008

AVATAR FASHION 2008

AVATAR FASHION 2008

AVATAR FASHION 2008

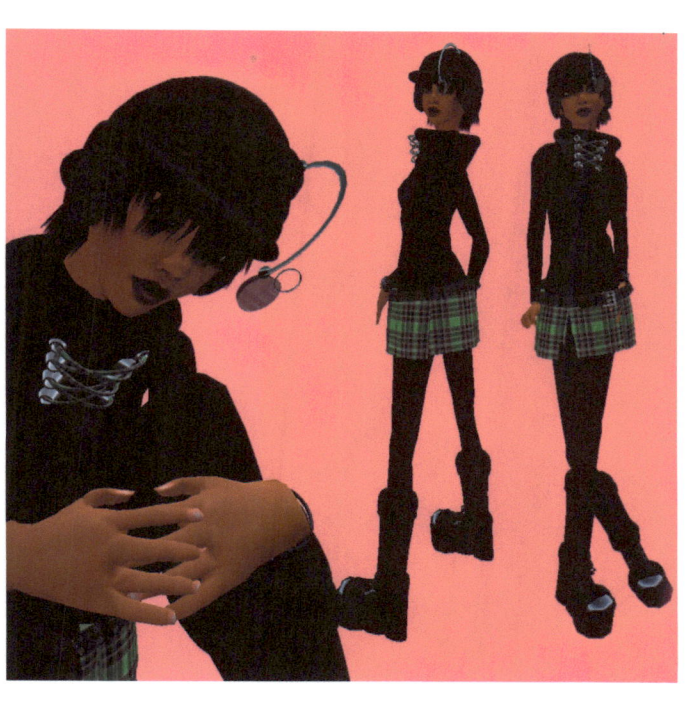

AVATAR FASHION 2008

www.acediaalbion.com
www.studiosfo.com

AVATAR FASHION 2008

www.ingramcontent.com/pod-product-compliance
Lightning Source LLC
Chambersburg PA
CBHW041539220426
43663CB00002B/78